RADICAL
EVANGELISM

Also available in the Pioneer *Perspectives* series:

Prophecy in the Church   Martin Scott
Relationships—Jesus Style   Stuart Lindsell
The Role and Ministry of Women   Martin Scott

For further information on the Pioneer *Perspectives* series and Pioneer, please write to:

P.O. Box 79c, Esher, Surrey, KT10 9LP

RADICAL EVANGELISM

Pete Gilbert

WORD PUBLISHING

Word (UK) Ltd
Milton Keynes, England

WORD AUSTRALIA
Kilsyth, Victoria, Australia

WORD COMMUNICATIONS LTD
Vancouver, B.C., Canada

STRUIK CHRISTIAN BOOKS (PTY) LTD
Maitland, South Africa

ALBY COMMERCIAL ENTERPRISES PTE LTD
Balmoral Road, Singapore

CHRISTIAN MARKETING NEW ZEALAND LTD
Havelock North, New Zealand

JENSCO LTD
Hong Kong

SALVATION BOOK CENTRE
Malaysia

RADICAL EVANGELISM

Published by Word (UK) Ltd. / Pioneer 1992.

ISBN 0-85009-728-2 (Australia ISBN 1-86258-212-2)

Unless otherwise indicated, Scripture quotations are from the HOLY BIBLE, NEW INTERNATIONAL VERSION (NIV). Copyright © 1973, 1978, 1984 by International Bible Society.

Front cover illustration: *Descent from the Cross*, Rubens, courtesy of Bridgeman Art Library.

Reproduced, printed and bound in Great Britain for Word (UK) Ltd. by Clays Ltd., St Ives plc.

92 93 94 95 / 10 9 8 7 6 5 4 3 2 1

FOREWORD

Pioneer *Perspectives* are perhaps more than their title suggests!

They are carefully researched presentations of material, on important issues, appealing to thinking churches, creative leaders and responsible Christians.

Each *Perspective* pioneers in as much as it is at the cutting edge of biblical and theological issues. Each will continue to pioneer with new ideas, concepts and data drawn from Scripture, history and a contemporary understanding of both.

They are perspectives in as much as they aim to be an important contribution to the ongoing debate on issues such as women in ministry and leadership; prophets and prophecy in the church; biblical models of evangelism; integrating and discipling new believers; growing and building local churches and further perspectives on Christ's second coming.

Importantly, these studies use a journal style of presentation, and are written by people who are currently working out the implications of the issues they are writing about, in local churches. This is vital if we are to escape the dangerous fantasy of abstract theology without practical experience. They are not written to contribute to the paralysis of analysis—rather to feed, strengthen, nurture and inform so that we can be equipped to get God's will done, by networking the nations with the Gospel using all the resources that are available to us.

God's Word is always an event. How much we thank Him that He has left us an orderly account of what He wants us to believe, how He wants us to live, and what He wants us to do in order to bring heaven to the earth. As we embrace a better understanding of Scripture, rooted in local church, national and international mission, we shall become a part of the great eschatological purpose of bringing back the

King—not for a church defeated, cowering and retiring but for one which, despite colossal odds, pressures and persecutions, is faithful to her Lord and His word. To do that we must 'search the Scriptures' to see if many of these 'new things' are true. I commend these *Perspectives* to you as they are published on a regular basis throughout these coming years.

Gerald Coates
Director Pioneer Trust/Team Leader

Pioneer consists of a team and network of churches, committed to dynamic and effective biblical Christianity.

The national team act as advisers and consultants to churches, which in many cases develop into a partnership with the Pioneer team. These are the churches keen to identify with the theology, philosophy, ethos and purpose of Pioneer. The team have a vigorous youth ministry, church-planting strategy and evangelistic emphasis.

Training courses include Equipped to Lead, Emerging Leaders and the highly successful TIE teams (Training In Evangelism).

Pioneer have also been instrumental in initiating and funding March for Jesus (with Ichthus/YWAM); Jubilee Campaign (for the suffering church worldwide); and ACET (Aids Care Education Training).

ACKNOWLEDGEMENTS

With grateful thanks to my wife Nikki and my daughter Freddie.

In writing this journal I would like to acknowledge Steve Clifford, Roger Forster and Roger Ellis for their timely, helpful and thought-provoking input. Thank you.

Pete Gilbert
May 1992

CONTENTS

CONTENTS

CHAPTER 1

THE THEOLOGY OF EVANGELISM

Theism or Deism?

The theology of evangelism rests squarely on the biblical notion that theism rather than deism dominates the universe. With some 72–80% of the population of the UK self-professing deists, it is important to note the distinction.

Deism boasts a world view which allows for a God of initiation, not of involvement. Thus, a deist will profess a belief in God, but not live as though God were involved and relevant, and certainly not know the God that he professes to believe in. To the deist, God, having started everything as a kind of divine principle of First Causes, is now remote, removed and uninvolved.

Theism, on the other hand, propagates a world view wherein God not only initiates but remains involved at every level, from the cosmic to the individual. The theist believes in a God who is everywhere, but also a God who is somewhere; Emmanuel, God with us. The God of the theist can be known, wants to be known, takes the initiative in being known, and remains intimately involved in His creation.

It is from this position of theism that a biblical theology of evangelism derives its basis and its dynamic. If God be involved with His creation, we can ask the following three questions:

- Does He choose to communicate with His creatures?
- How does He do so?

- And with what message would He have us encompass His creation?

The answers to these questions are respectively:

- 'Yes'
- 'Incarnationally'
- 'The Gospel'

The assurance of these three statements becomes the backdrop to any theology of evangelism.

The God Who Communicates

Scripture, itself one foundational means of communication from God to people, gives clear indication throughout that we serve a God eager to communicate with people. He created people in His image (Genesis 1:26) at the pinnacle of unfallen created order, wherein everything else was 'good', but people were 'very good' (Genesis 1:4, 10, 12, 18, 21, 25 and 31). It is evident that we were made to enjoy God and be enjoyed by Him (Genesis 1:28).

God did not create us out of any sense of need within the Godhead, for God was already in perfect relationship within the first family of the Godhead; Father, Son and Holy Spirit (the 'us' of Genesis 1:26). But God made us out of a heart of extravagant creativity and love—a desire to share and relate.

All relationships demand communication and so God walked and talked with Adam in the cool of the evening in an unfallen paradise (Genesis 3:8). Nor should we be surprised that God is a communicator when we observe the same desires to share love, vocalise it and demonstrate it in ourselves, as we are made in the image of God (we, as He, have thoughts, desires, emotions, personality, a will, and are communicators)—communication is not the result of the Fall!

Incarnational Communication

If God is a communicator and does communicate, then
we must look for the evidence of what He communicates and how He does this *throughout* Scripture,
although the principle of *'first* mention' is an
important one. (Following this principle we look for
the context and content of the *original* place where, for
example in this instance, God as a communicator
appears.) Using the principle of first mention
means we will avoid basing our theology on
correctives alone—it would, for example, be wise to
build a theology of practice of church life on the
Gospels and on Acts, more than on the Epistles,
which *are* largely corrective.

Thus Genesis, the book of beginnings, indicates the
God who communicates. The rest of Scripture not
only confirms this, but demonstrates *how* God
communicates. One would expect God to use the best
methods, and this He does in choosing incarnational
communication. God's ultimate message is of who He
is, and so His ultimate communication is of Himself:
God does not have a message, He *is* the message.

God, in His dealings through human history, has
always wrapped His message up in a visual display.
So His heart of love and desire to communicate gets
wrapped up in a body—and Adam and Eve make
their appearance. When later God desires to
communicate He chooses a people, Israel, to embody
His nature. When Israel drifts from this destiny God
chooses prophets to speak and to demonstrate His will,
using visual aids as varied as potters' wheels, clay jars,
piles of dung, streaking naked through the streets,
marriage to a prostitute, etc. When they are
ignored, the God who communicates goes silent for
400 years between the Old and New Testaments, only
speaking again just prior to His supreme act of
communication, now through the prophet John the
Baptist.

This is one reason why people flocked out into the

desert to hear John, because suddenly God was communicating again, and now He was preparing people for the pivotal point of human history, when the Word of God would become flesh. God would wrap Himself up in human flesh and become man, incarnational communication par excellence; Jesus Christ (Hebrews 1:1–3). And this God-Man, Jesus Christ the Son of God, used the same principle of communication as His Father: He didn't bring good news, He *is* good news.

Jesus only ever equated Himself with two things— according to Jesus both God the Father *and* the Gospel were both the same thing as Jesus the Son (Mark 8:35 and Mark 10:29). And Jesus' teaching methods are the equivalent of the Old Testament prophets, full of visual aids and actions to demonstrate the gospel of the Kingdom. Hence the parables, the fig tree, the fishers of men, the coin of Caesar, breathing on His disciples. Also, the healings and deliverances of the gospels and of Acts become another part of incarnational communication, a fleshing out of the message, a confirmation of its authenticity, and a demonstration of the supernatural nature of God's gospel of the Kingdom.

Luke makes the connection clear in writing to Theophilus in Acts 1:1—'. . . all that Jesus began to *do* and to *teach* . . .' And after Jesus' death and resurrection the Holy Spirit continues to communicate in the same incarnational way—He lives *in* people now (whereas in the Old Testament He came *upon* people), and Jesus' disciples, followers of the Way (John 14:6), become Christians or, literally, 'little Christs', who are to go on being filled with the Holy Spirit (Ephesians 5:18). This again is incarnational communication—God got His will done in the body of Jesus Christ on earth, a body filled with God's Holy Spirit (Luke 4:1).

Now God gets His will done through the second body of Jesus Christ on earth, made up of 'little Christs', and also filled with God's Holy Spirit. The Holy Spirit continues to communicate God's heart to God's world incarnationally, hence the continuation of signs and wonders, of healings, deliverances and miracles, of prophecies, tongues and interpretations, of visions and dreams, and of social action. This is incarnational communication.   Just as with the first (human/physical) body of Jesus Christ on earth, so too this second body of Christ, the church, doesn't just have the message, it embodies the message, lives and demonstrates it. Incarnational communication has the advantage of reducing the risk of distortion during transmission of the message.

The Message of Good News

So the biblical base for the theology of evangelism thus far rests on the contention that

1. God is a communicator (theism and not deism), and that
2. His means of communication is incarnational, rather than merely didactic.

The third propositional base for a theology of evangelism is that the content of the gospel is good news; if the message *is* God (Father, Son and Holy Spirit) and if God *is* Love, the God of Peace (1 John 4:8, 1 Corinthians 14:33) then the message will be one of Love and Peace—loving God and being at peace with Him, and therefore loving others and being at peace with them (1 John 3:14–16), as we have also learned to love and be at peace with ourselves (Luke 10:27). And, indeed we will discover, when we later look at the content of the gospel, that this summary is a fair one.

CHAPTER 2

THE BIBLICAL BASE FOR A THEOLOGY OF EVANGELISM

How consistent is this biblical base for a theology of evangelism? Do we really have a mandate to incarnationally communicate good news?

Evangelism proper is a term which can only apply to the New Testament because of the specific words used; these terms will merit a word search following these introductory remarks of this *Perspective*. But the process of evangelism, the incarnational communication of God's good news, runs throughout the Old Testament as well, wherein it is more properly designated 'proselytisation'. Thus God created people to stand in the flow of His blessing (Genesis 1:28a) *and* to create more opportunities for God to bless (Genesis 1:28b). God chose Abraham to bless him and through him to create a chosen nation. However, this wasn't a chosen nation whom God would love to the exclusion of others; it was a nation chosen *for a purpose*, to bless *the nations* (Genesis 17).

God's heart has consistently been for the world, for all nations, for every people group (the *te ethne* of Matthew 28:16–20). God's original plan before the Fall (first mention!) was to bless all of creation and for people to represent God to all of creation. People were created to bless and be blessed. After the Fall God's covenant with Abraham was the same—he would be blessed and would bless all nations. This is made clear again and again throughout the Old Testament (Isaiah 42:6, 49:6, 52:10, Psalm 96) and is reflected in God's commands to the Jews concerning their treatment of and proselytisation amongst foreigners/sojourners/Gentiles of the other nations (e.g. Leviticus 25, Deuteronomy 24 and 25).

In the New Testament the same plan is at work, with Jesus Christ and His disciples incarnationally communicating with Jew and Gentile alike (Mark 7:24, Acts 10) and indeed the plan's completion being not only commanded (Matthew 28:16–20, Acts 1:8) but the return of Jesus Christ dependent upon its completion (Matthew 24:14, 2 Peter 3:9, Revelation 7:9).

Summary of the Basis for a Theology of Evangelism

1. God desires to communicate with all peoples of all times, at all times.
2. His methods of communication are incarnational; He embodies His message and character in His people.
3. God's character is good news, His message is good news.

These three tenets are observable from Scripture pre- and post-Fall, are effected by all three parts of the Godhead, Father, Son and Holy Spirit, and are still in operation through the Holy Spirit in the church.

Some New Testament Greek Words

It will be necessary and helpful to examine the specific New Testament Greek words which give rise to the term 'theology of evangelism'. Theology simply means 'knowledge of God and of His word' (*theos* = God, *logos* = word). Thus, a 'theology of . . .' refers to the teaching of God and His Word on that subject (e.g. a theology of soteriology would refer to an understanding of God's salvation plan; *soterio* = salvation, wholeness, healing).

The word 'evangelism' comes from the New

Testament word *euvangelion*. This word occurs many times in the New Testament (96 times, usually translated 'gospel') and is one borrowed by the contemporary New Testament writers. Some words in Scripture were particularly coined by their authors to describe features of Christianity that were radically, startlingly new, and for which no existing words could suffice (e.g. the 'one body' which is the new concept of church, encompassing as it did, according to God's proselytising plan, both Jew and Gentile, acquires the newly coined word *sunsoma*). But *euvangelion* was a word already in existence in first-century Greek. The word had a specific meaning.

Imagine the not unfamiliar scenario in the first-century Middle East, in which a city is under threat from a militant enemy. As the enemy's army approaches the city, the city guards are sent out to engage the enemy in battle while they are yet some miles distant. The city waits anxiously to hear whether their army has been successful or not, whether or not they have been delivered from their aggressors. Finally, a herald returns to the city, a messenger from the city guard. He carries victory news; the enemy has been routed, the city is safe, its people's lives spared, their freedom ensured. This news is the *euvangelion*; its literal meaning—'life-changing good news of a military victory'—with all the inherent implications of deliverance, safety, freedom and celebration.

The word *euvangelion* gives us the word 'evangelism' and the Old English translation of *euvangelion* is 'godspell', meaning more simply 'good news', and from which we derive the word 'gospel' (and the title of Lloyd-Webber's musical *Godspell*!).

The herald, messenger or proclaimer of this news would be the *euvangelistes*, from which we derive the word 'evangelist'. Unlike *euvangelion*, this word occurs only three times in the New Testament. In developing a theology of evangelism one might wish for a more frequent word use than this; if God is so committed to communicating good news incarnationally, shouldn't the word for those who, as little Christs, now proclaim the good news, be used more often? An examination of the three times *euvangelistes*/'evangelist' occurs in the New Testament will shed some light on this apparent anomaly.

CHAPTER 3

EVANGELISTS IN THE NEW TESTAMENT

1. Philip

The first time the word occurs is in Acts in reference to 'Philip the evangelist'. The context is revealing. Philip makes his first appearance in Acts 8:26 when, led from the revival at the birth of the church in Jerusalem, he is supernaturally transported (such is the importance of this event) into the desert region around Gaza. Many of the readers of Luke's narrative in Acts would register that the desert is the place of God's justice, where wrath and forgiveness are combined, and is often the scene for confrontation between the agents of God and of Satan (Luke 4).

With all this as background Philip has his monumental meeting with the Ethiopian official. The reception of the gospel by this latter results in an incarnational act—baptism. And Philip, having apparently fulfilled his task, returns to Jerusalem in the same way that he came and, as far as can be ascertained from church history, this episode was what brought the gospel via Ethiopia (Old Testament Cush) into the continent of Africa. Of such significance was this encounter.

Yet this is *not* the incident when Philip is referred to as Philip the evangelist. Rather, it is some 13 chapters and 17 years later, in Acts 21:8–9. By now Philip is a recognised part of a local church, accountable to leadership there, enjoying apostolic input (from Paul and team). Furthermore, his family is in order, his daughters are prophetesses and it is now that *euvan-*

gelistes, so sparingly and carefully used in the New Testament, is applied to Philip. Could these factors of local church base, accountability, relationship, family and lifestyle, apostolic framework, be significant in this choice of words? The second example of the use of the word 'evangelist' indicates that they may be.

2. Paul's Letter to the Ephesians

In Ephesians 4:11–13 Paul lists a number of ministry giftings. This is not the only place where those ministries appear together (see 1 Corinthians 12:28), though, rather like the Holy Spirit's grace gifts (the *charismata* of 1 Corinthians 12—14, and Romans 12:6–8), the different lists do not appear to be intended as complete or exhaustive. The word 'ministry' simply means 'area of work or service'; consequently one's ministry can be correctly defined as one's life, those areas of service around which there will be a cluster of gifts both natural and supernatural, with perhaps a particular emphasis to the fore. Thus the evangelist will love to serve the body of Christ and unbelievers by explaining God's gospel in such a manner that a decision for or against is often necessary, natural and desirable.

The evangelist's natural gifting will tend to make him or her very interested in life and in people and therefore an interesting person, with a degree of extroversion quite likely. This supernatural gifting ought best to include the gifts of healing, word of knowledge, word of wisdom, gift of distinguishing of spirits, faith, teaching, and the prophetic—this cluster of *charismata* will achieve many of the jobs that the evangelist will embark upon.

It will be helpful to note that God uses a blending of natural and supernatural giftings in the individual to produce ministry from the life of that individual. God is even able to use weakness as well as strengths. The risks of creating stereotypes in describing evangelists in this manner are outweighed by our need to understand how and why the evangelist functions.

It is my opinion, both from experience and observation, that many evangelists go into evangelism from a starting point of insecurity. A part of the role of the evangelist is easily assessable in terms of performance, of success or failure; that is to say, people either get saved or they don't. A frequent (though often subconscious) initial motivation for the evangelist is the need to prove their self-worth to God and to others by demonstrating the effectiveness of their ministry in terms of 'numbers saved'. The sense of urgency which drives many evangelists will also often cause them to be both impatient and workaholic in nature. The desire to be out on the edge in the interface between church and world will also sometimes cause them to be individualists and can exacerbate a tendency toward isolationism and independence.

Anointed evangelists will be people with faith and vision, and their anointing will always provoke action rather than passivity, with an ability to rock the status quo, particularly in terms of religion, tradition, ritual, and means of communication. Their desire to communicate with as many different types of people as possible will tend to make them both gregarious and sometimes outspoken. Furthermore, the fact that their anointing means that they do have ultimate spiritual answers to the deepest needs of individuals (i.e. the need for salvation and the knowledge of God) does tend to give evangelists the impression that they have the answers to all life's questions, constantly making them experts in most fields!

Any evangelist worth their salt and growing in their anointing will also have a heart being constantly stretched by God's Holy Spirit in terms of compassion and sensitivity, and the dual tug of the sensitive and the brash often lies at the heart of the character of many evangelists. These factors of strength and weakness make it all the more important that the evangelist is not only recognised for his or her character and gifting, but embraced into team (church) and given a head alongside the other church-based ministries.

The Ephesians 4 passage outlines five particular ministries which Paul notes as foundational to the building of the church. The ministry gifts are given to the church by the Spirit of Jesus, a specific emphasis different to the emphasis of 1 Corinthians 12—14, where the giver of gifts is the Holy Spirit. The emphasis on the Spirit of Jesus is because the church is built by Jesus, not by the evangelist, or the apostle, prophet, etc. Jesus' promise (Matthew 16:18) is to build His church. His command was for His disciples to seek the Kingdom (Matthew 6:33).

So, the right to determine the design, shape and structure of the church belongs to Jesus—it remains His church and His to build. Jesus' disciples get on with seeking the Kingdom of God, wherever the rule of King Jesus is expressed in and through His kingdom people. The church remains the principal agent through which God brings His Kingdom about on earth (a Kingdom which is at hand, which is within you, which is to come on earth as in Heaven). Yet the Kingdom of God is bigger/wider than the church as it permeates through education, health, social services, industry, media, entertainments, etc. This Kingdom emphasis is a critical one in radical evangelism—it is the focus which will keep the church turning outward, staying relevant, remaining involved. Again it is a focus to which we must return if our evangelism is to be radical.

Ephesians 4 makes it very clear that these five-fold ministries (some might prefer four-fold by combining the roles of pastor and teacher, though both functions and giftings have very different emphases and are, in my opinion, separate ministries), since they are foundational to building the church, are therefore all expansionist ministries. Many of the parables of the Kingdom are growth parables, and three key parabolic components of growth (e.g. Luke 8:5–15) are also found here in Ephesians: the first is that growth is *qualitative*, the second that it is *quantitative*, and the third that it is *growth by multiplication* and not by addition.

The church, the primary vehicle of the Kingdom, is no different; although many parts (Romans 12, 1 Corinthians 14), it *is* one body (Ephesians 2:16) and created for qualitative, quantitative, multiplied growth. Thus the often stated notion that the evangelist and the pastor are antithetical, that the one is the 'accelerator pedal', whilst the latter is the 'brake pedal', must be abandoned as unbiblical. *All* the five-fold ministry gifts are growth-orientated, none are maintenance-minded, all are gifts to the whole church.

Responsible evangelism necessitates making disciples (Matthew 28:16–20), which requires pastoral input. The evangelist gets the people out of Egypt, and the pastor gets Egypt out of the people! The evangelist needs the pastor who is thinking growth, maturity, character, discipling. The pastor needs the evangelist who is thinking new birth, friendship networks (friendship evangelism is really exercising non-religious pastoral skills on non-Christians!), numbers of new people to be discipled.

So, the *euvangelistes* mentioned in Ephesians 4 is given along *with* the other four ministries for the building up of the church, through multiplication. The role of the evangelist is to equip the saints, for *their* works of service (ministries). This clearly indicates the two-fold role of the evangelist—to both *do* evangelism and to *train/equip* the church to do evangelism.

When the New Testament refers to church it is with a localised expression in mind (i. e. the church at Corinth, Colossae, Philippi, etc.) not *just* a theoretical concept of the church universal. The evangelist is given to train and equip the *local* church, first his/her own, and, perhaps in an apostolic team context, to do the same trans-locally. Apostolic *team* is vital for this as the church is built on the five-fold ministries—the lone-wolf itinerant evangelist is unbiblical, outmoded, an aberration. This, of course, is as true for the one who is a prophet without any church context, as for the apostle who is unaccountable; or for the unbiblical use of the title 'Pastor' to denote a one-man ministry who leads a church, as opposed to one part of a five-fold ministry-gifted team.

As well as working in a team, any evangelist who seeks only to *do* evangelism, whilst omitting the aspects of teaching, training, imparting and equipping the saints, will quickly reach the limits of their effectiveness (which will usually be the capacity of their diary). Any evangelist who merely teaches and trains others without hands-on practice and contemporary experience in reality loses the right to train—biblical discipleship links training with doing, just as real theology affects lifestyle. Neither of these two extremes is biblical; in scripture the evangelist is one who *does*, and who *facilitates* others to do, evangelism. The second mention of evangelist is, like the first, in the context of church.

3. Paul's Second Letter to Timothy

The third and final time the word makes its appearance in the Greek New Testament is in 2 Timothy 4 :1–5, and the context is instruction to a dearly loved disciple on how to relate to and function in church. It is within this context of church that Paul addresses a specific directive to his acolyte Timothy: 'Do the work of an evangelist.' The emphasis here is on the proclamatory work of the evangelist, 'preaching the word in and out of season', and also that evangelism *is* work, albeit enjoyable work.

There is an indication from the text that Timothy, even if not an evangelist, is to do the work/ job/service of one—a lesson for those in the church who might propagate the notion that to do evangelism is someone else's job because it's not their ministry!

It is worth noting in this final use of the word *euvangelistes* that Paul was addressing Timothy, the leader of a New Testament resource church (one which would plant other churches again and again and continue to resource those churches with ministry and finance), covering some 25,000 people! And early church history indicates that Timothy would have been around 17–19 years old at the time. Evangelism, church leadership, the work of the evangelist and youth can, and do, all go together in the New Testament. These references (Acts 21:8–9, Ephesians 4:11–13 and 2 Timothy 4:1–5) mark, then, the only three uses of the word *euvangelistes* in the New Testament.

CHAPTER 4

EVANGELISM AND CHURCH HISTORY

Thus far the New Testament has been allowed to portray a view of evangelism which is normative; evangelism which reflects the good news of the God of the Bible who wishes to speak to all peoples, by demonstrating the good news *in and through* His church. A word search thus far has strengthened this notion of *church-based* evangelism.

This *Perspective* refers to radical evangelism in this respect—that evangelism needs to regain its New Testament roots (Latin *radix,* root, radical). Such evangelism will be radical precisely because church history has unfortunately consigned evangelism to a position of peripheral influence, both in the lives of individual Christians and of their collective church experience. Evangelism has been separated from its roots within church life.

Church and State

Historically the reason for evangelistic marginalisation lies in the fourth century, when the Roman Empire became the Holy Roman Empire with the alleged conversion of the Emperor Constantine. The church, which until then not only had been separate from the state, its power, its politics, and its wealth, but largely persecuted by that state, now became wedded to the state. The effects were far reaching; the Roman army were to convert *en masse* on pain of death by beheading—an interesting fourth-century evangelistic technique!

From an early church built on the blood of its martyrs, emerged a church increasingly influenced by decisions of government. Originally pacifist by principle, the church now saw increasing advantage in Holy or Just Warfare against the enemies of that State. Wealth once given away and evenly distributed became a part of power politics. The Kingdom of God became confused with the kingdoms of man and the power of the church. The Dark Ages lay ahead of the church as the light and the urgency of the gospel were dimmed, though never put out (John 1:5).

Clergy and Laity

The distinction between clergy and laity also marked this period in the church's history, although neither term is biblical. The words derive from the Greek *klerikos* meaning 'member' and *laos* meaning 'people', so that in reality *all* disciples are *both* the clergy and laity of God and His church!

An important part of both the theology and the practice of evangelism is this priesthood of all believers. The distinction between people and leaders, between committed and nominal, grew throughout church history, however, and a very peculiar view of church emerged.

By the time of the Reformation Luther thought that church was wherever the 'preaching of the word' occurred. Zwingli added 'the practice of the sacraments' to that, and Calvin added discipline, as was his wont! The committed and trained professionals became the clergy, and the people became the pew-fodder. Little real attention has since been paid to the theology of church, and many have not got beyond these Reformation concepts, stressing as they did individual salvation at the expense of corporate life and responsibility.

From the fourth century, nominalism then swept into the Christian Church; the tares and wheat, the fish of all kinds in the parables of Matthew 13 coexisted together in the *church* instead of in the *kingdom* (as the parable actually maintains), and one result of this distinction of clergy/laity was the marginal-isation of the church activists. And so in the Middle Ages, if an individual felt the call of God and wanted to serve society around him, he had to become full-time (clergy) and often then would have to work out his call monastically. The picture emerges of keen activists removed from the life of the local church in the community and into the specific life of the monasteries. Many of these monastic orders were good in and of themselves, active socially, in a kind of Middle-Age church planting, as they sought to reproduce themselves in their work with the poor and the sick, but the damage had been done. In effect, local church had become pastoral and maintenance-orientated, credal and sacramental, and the evangelistic, socially involved disciples of Jesus existed separately in their own specific enclaves.

The eighteenth and nineteenth centuries saw a further development of this marginalisation of what should be the mission of the whole church, with the formation of the great missionary movements in an unbroken line and move of the Holy Spirit (evidence for God getting His will done either despite the church or because of it?) linking Count Zinzendorf to the Moravians, John Wesley to William Carey's Missionary Society formed in 1792. By the end of the nineteenth century world Christianity had increased by 4%, yet still evangelistic fervour was largely out-worked in the mission field, outside the life of the local church.

Evangelism in Modern Times

The twentieth century saw little change until its closing years. The missionary movement has had its parallel in the development of para-church organisa-tions (like YWAM, OM, Horizons, BYFC). Many of these para-church organisations often have an emphasis on youth, which reflects both God's heart to involve young people, and the radical zealousness of committed

Christian youth. Such movements are frequently staffed by activists and evangelists who often at best believe in church, but have been frustrated by a lack of properly working New Testament church models, and who at worst won't be held accountable by local church life and relationships. Many of them carry a real sense of God's call upon their lives, but are bereft of a context (church) within which to work that call out, and are potentially frustrated at the still dominant 'professionalism' (clergy/laity distinctions again) which many church denominations exercise, whereby service of God demands middle-class management systems, three years at Bible college and a theology degree! This is truly devangelism, emptying the church by degrees!

Indeed, with the vicious onslaught of liberal Christianity, highjacking involvement in the social aspects of the Gospel, but denying its power, and having at its heart the deathwish ability to empty British churches by the thousand, it became evident that many evangelicals between 1830 and the 1960s, as enlightenment, rationalism and post-Kantian human consciousness became prevalent, retreated into para-church activism or behind dogma and doctrines, and became too timid for evangelistic activity. Thus the twentieth century spawned a kind of Greek philosophical version of evangelicalism, wherein one could be evangelical by persuasion, but not evangelistic in purpose; one's beliefs no longer affecting one's actions.

In Jewish thought (reflected in Scripture also) there is no separation between hearing and doing, between belief and action, nor between secular and spiritual. The Old Testament had its priests and its people, but the New Testament has its priesthood of all believers. In Jewish thought the gospel, if really heard, leads to renewed lifestyle of all God's people, and encompasses every part of their lifestyles. This leaves no room for churches which are evangelical by name but not by nature. Jim Wallis, American Christian theologian and practitioner, expresses it well in a pithy turn of phrase: 'What you *do* on Monday morning is what you really believe; everything else is religion!' This is 'religion' of the worst kind, adopting an outward form and denying the power, leading to hypocrisy (Matthew 23), failure and disillusionment.

However, in the last third of this century evangelism has come back firmly onto the agenda of many local, national and international churches, and in many ways the UK is in a unique position to be used of God in establishing the priority and agenda of evangelism in local church life. The Pentecostal movement of the first half of the century has given way to the Charismatic movement of the 1960s, the Renewal movement of the 1970s across the established denominational churches, and in the 80s and 90s the continued emergence of the New (or house) Church streams, many of which after a period of strategic introversion (finding the Holy Spirit, body life, praise and worship, discovering one another, spiritual warfare, etc.) are now thoroughly involved in evangelism, and seeing primary growth (a minimum 60% of total) through conversion.

These networks of Spirit-filled, unreligious, socially aware, apostolically planted new churches, whilst not the sole agent for evangelism in this nation, do offer the best hope for seeing the nation evangelised according to the vision of movements across churches like Challenge 2000 (aiming at 20% of England to be Christian by the year AD 2000), March for Jesus, the Decade of Evangelism, etc. Few other countries in Europe, if any, have the strength of these networks, particularly when it comes to church planting: the UK has much to give away, yet also much to do.

When it comes to evangelism, there is much to catch up with globally; there are more Christians alive *now* than the total of Christians who have lived throughout the whole of history. Something like 63–80,000 people a day are becoming Christians, and in some nations like Korea, with the three largest churches in the world (the largest at 700,000) the conversion rate is outstripping the birth rate! In Chile 47% of the population are Christians, in Brazil 50%, in Guetemala 48%. Globally some 1200 new Christian churches are planted each week. Fifty years ago China had only a few thousand Christians; conservative estimates now place the number of believers at 50–70 million, with 23,000 new converts each day!

Yet even in Europe the Holy Spirit is moving, with new churches planted in France, an unprecedented move of God upon the youth of Germany, Eastern Europe open as never before to the Gospel, even Albania (once the most Godless country on earth) experiencing church growth. The world church is currently expanding at a rate of 8% per annum. If we can increase that to 11%, then by AD 2000 we can have planted one church for every 1500 head of population, a target that will assist the overall goal of evangelism to tell 'all the nations' (the people groups— *te ethne*—ethnic groups, of Matthew 28:16–20) the good news of Jesus Christ in an observable, accessible, culturally relevant (incarnated) way.

There are some 12,000 unreached people groups to go, but at the end of the first century AD there were 60,000. And then the proportion of non-Christians to Christians was 360 to 1. Now it's down to 7 to 1, and by AD 2000 the estimate is as low as 4 to 1. 34% of the world's population are now practising Christians. Christianity remains the largest and fastest growing of the world's major religions. A return to radical evangelism which is *from* a church base, to *plant* a church base, will exacerbate this growth.

This encouragement is needed, for we are seeking to reverse a trend which in England between 1979 and 1989 has emptied churches at the alarming rate of 1,000 people per week. Yet whilst all the major denominations have declined in that period, the Pentecostals haven't, and the New Churches are growing at a staggering rate, with around one thousand churches in 25 networks, involving 250,000 people and seeing two new churches planted each week. The means has been radical evangelism, back to the roots of church-based training and doing. Some of the lessons of history have been learned—unless we learn by the mistakes of our history we are likely to repeat that history. It is time for a new look at the old Commission.

CHAPTER 5

THE WHY OF CHURCH-BASED EVANGELISM—I

In the next two chapters we will look at twelve reasons why evangelism must be local church-based in nature. Church-based evangelism is *not* to preclude specialist groups working across churches, or mass evangelism with churches working together, but it *is* to place the apostolic input, emphasis, style, initiative (manpower, finances, etc.) and results firmly *within* the context of local church (already existing or to be planted).

These same twelve hallmarks can be summarised as the four great criteria that the Jews expected would herald the coming Messiah:

- that God would be present and immediate again,
- that Satan would be defeated,
- that salvation would come,
- that all this would create a gospel people.

Ironically church is, of course, the New Israel—the place where those criteria are ushered in and fulfilled by Christ. Why must New Testament (and therefore radical) evangelism be church-based?

1. Church is *God's means of incarnational communication*. It is church which roots God's people as a community within communities, as localised, accessible, and demonstrably as family, given all families derive their name (i.e. scripturally find their

identity) from the Father of all (Ephesians 3:14). Church alone allows for a proper cultural contextualisation of evangelism, where the means of evangelism used in Bognor will be different from those used in Cobham, and different again in Tooting. Church, made up as it is of people living, working and socialising in their community, is the best means of making communication of the gospel relevant to that community.

2. Church then becomes *a model mitigating against the credibility gap* which much evangelism exposes. The question 'Do I have to go to church to be a Christian?' in the mouths of 11–16-year-olds becomes the statement 'I'm no better or worse than that lot down the road in the local church—a load of hypocrites *they* are!' later on in life. The accusation is all too often justifiably levelled. Yet real church (Acts 2:42–47) built apostolically on relationships, teaching, signs and wonders, praise and worship, prayer and evangelism, counters this and becomes a demonstration of what one believes, so that when our lifestyle demands an explanation and positive questions are asked of us at work, we can answer and point towards a corporate demonstration: 'This is *how* I live, this is *why* I live this way, here's *where* you can see it in action.'

3. Church is *the only known New Testament context across which the five-fold ministry gifts* (on which Jesus builds His church) *flow*. The resources of apostle, prophet, evangelist, pastor and teacher are all vital to church planting and church growth and are the team within which the evangelists function, as they equip the saints and do the work of evangelism. (See the previous examination of Ephesians 4:11–13.) Church as a body will have most of the gifts needed for evangelism, and where help is needed from outside the local area, the context should again be across churches linked apostolically.

4. There is a real sense in which church must be *a prophetic demonstration* not only to the angelic forces

(1 Peter 1:10–12) but also *to the nations*. In embodying all kinds of people with varying background, race, age, class, etc., church is heterogeneous. Evangelism works best across like peer-groups (homogeneous), but that is an evangelistic tool, and should not be confused with church. Church is a microcosm of the Kingdom of God (Galatians 3:28, Colossians 3:11, Romans 10:12, Revelations 7:9) and all church should be Kingdom (though not all that is Kingdom will be church).

5. Church gives *a profile to the people of God in a vicinity* in a way that organisations or individuals cannot. Church demonstrates the unity of the body of Christ, which exists on two levels—the 'mystical' inherent unity of being born of one Spirit which is one body, described in 1 Corinthians 12. Specifically and importantly, local church demonstrates the unity of the Holy Spirit which is to be 'maintained', worked out and worked at (Ephesians 4:2). This is a more tangible expression (through relationships primarily, not through projects or ecumenical committees) of the unity that Jesus prayed for and which He maintained would demonstrate to the world that we belong to the Father (John 17). The profile is necessary to a living demonstration of the Kingdom of God, which church is.

6. Because church is team, church is *a safe environment within which to train and do evangelism,* and in which to make mistakes, recognising that mistakes (a) are not sin, and will be covered (b) by God, and (c) by other team/church members. The strengths of one will cover the weaknesses of others in evangelism. This is part of the vital link between our church relationships and our evangelism—we are seen in our unity to belong to God and we therefore fight together, hence Ephesians 6 on spiritual warfare (part of evangelism) following on the teaching on relationships (church and family) in Ephesians 5.

7. Church life provides *a network of mutual submission* (Ephesians 5:21 where *hupeiko* means 'open to

persuasion') *and servant leadership* (Mark 10:42–45) within which each member is accountable. Accountability (whole lifestyle—actions, words, time, money, morality, etc.) is a key factor in evangelism. It keeps church on target and stops lone-wolf itinerant evangelistic 'snipers', instead focusing the body as a *fighting unit* with common aims and purpose. Accountability makes maximum use of resources (Where does the evangelist/evangelism team work next and how? What is the evangelism budget? What happens to converts? etc.), and helps shape and develop those resources.

Accountability also guards against the world's perception of individual, independent cranks. The world looks with justifiable suspicion on the individual, lonely voice in the High Street, but is compelled by the unity and drive of a group clearly representing many diverse people. This is the weight behind the command of Hebrews 10:25. It's not an argument for might is right, but it is a response to 'beware the loner' and a vindication of 'heed the group'.

Across local churches the Evangelical Alliance has been able to give such a corporate voice to in excess of 1,000,000 evangelical Christians, but the strength lies not in the individual members (except perhaps financially for the E.A.) but in the churches represented by those individuals. With accountability comes authority. Authority is sorely needed in evangelism (over Satan, sickness, suffering and sin) and in order to have and exercise authority one must be under authority (Matthew 8:5–13).

8. Much evangelism has suffered in the past from inconsistency (of content and approach) and lack of persistency (geographic or demographic areas), subsequently gaining for itself the reputation of a 'hit or miss, hit and run' nature. Church guards against this, because by its nature church is *consistently rooted in an area* and able to refine and develop her evangelistic strategies and methods. And church should have short- (one year), medium- (five to ten years), and long-term (twenty-five years plus) evangelistic goals, of

which more later—these will prohibit church from lacking in persistency as it distinguishes between hard and soft areas for evangelism, and between sowing and reaping activities—also see later.

9.   Church is *the best channel for prayer, praise and worship*.   All are possible on an individual basis, but when Christians come together in prayer, praise and worship, the result is greater than the sum of the parts in the release of spiritual dynamics (*dunamis*—'power of God') and of faith. So when two or more agree together, Jesus answers their prayers (Matthew 18:19). And when Christians are together in unity, God commands blessings (Psalm 133), and inhabits their praises (Psalm 22:3 KJV). Since prayer, praise and worship are vital in evangelism, as we will explore later, then the measure by which church facilitates the one, will be the measure by which it effects the other.

CHAPTER 6

THE WHY OF CHURCH-BASED EVANGELISM—II

10. Church is *necessary to evangelism if that radical evangelism is to be good news of the Kingdom of God*, as Jesus commanded (Matthew 10). What is the content of His gospel, its essential *kerugma*? It is good news (God's creation was 'good'), then bad news (people foul it up), then good news (God sends His Son Jesus to pay the price—the perfect covers the imperfect). The atonement is vicarious (done for us), propitiary (an appeasement for sin before a Holy God, in the face of a vengeful and legalistic Satan, restoring the human dignity of mankind, a three-way atonement), substitutionary (in place of us). The atonement restores oneness with God through expiation of sin, resulting in justification (a 'straightening' of our standing before God in Christ) and sanctification (changing lifestyle).

Perhaps best summed up by John 3:16, the *kerugma* has God as initiator ('For God . . .' see Romans 5:8) of a message of love and good news ('so loved . . .') for all people ('the world . . .') centred around Jesus ('that he gave his one and only Son . . .') such that belief in Him leading to action (James 2:14–26; 'that whoever believes in Him . . .') will lead to salvation *from* Hell *to* Heaven now *and* eternally ('shall not perish but have eternal life.'). The constituent parts of this good news are:

10.a) **Words**—*Euvangelion* is 'good news which is

heralded or proclaimed', and consequently the gospel
is referred to in the New Testament by a number of
Greek verbs relating to the use of *words* as an inherent
part of evangelism. The most commonly used are
diamarturathai (to testify), *karagallein* (to proclaim),
keruasein (to herald), *diderkeai* (to teach), *dialegestahi* (to
argue), *apologia* (to reason).

10.b) **Wonders**—an integral part of the gospel. Jesus
spoke more about healing than about forgiveness—one
can omit *neither* from the gospel of the Kingdom. God
chose the arena of the supernatural to demonstrate His
Kingdom and the Sonship of Jesus Christ. These
wonders of healings and deliverance following faith
(14 occasions in Mark's gospel alone, 25% of the total
content of the gospels, 30% with the book of Acts), are
signs of the Kingdom (Mark 16:17) and are integral to
the gospel because they are necessary for *total*
evangelisation in extent and content (Romans 15:18–19,
Luke 4:18); because they demonstrate the gospel as a
visual aid (1 Corinthians 2:4–5); they confirm its
content (Mark 16:9–16); they give the gospel profile
attesting toward it (Hebrews 2:4), and they
authenticate the gospel as the real item—accept no
substitutes! (2 Corinthians 12:12) The term 'wonders'
includes the miraculous (for example Philip's
transportation in Acts 8, the sorcerer's blindness in
Acts 13, Ananias and Sapphira in Acts 5, the
multiplication miracles of John 6, etc.) but majors on
healing (Luke 10:9, Luke 4:18–19) and deliverance
(Matthew 12:28–29).

Such signs and wonders are included in the Great
Commission of Matthew 28:16–20, referred to in the
sub-title of this *Perspective*, by implication of
multiplication (i.e. 'everything I have commanded
you' must include Matthew 10:7–8, etc.). They are
among the great works promised by Jesus (where
'works' specifically means miracles/healings, see John
4:34, 5:20–36, 7:3–21, 9:33, 10:25–32, 15:24), in John
14:11–14, and are a destruction of the works of the
enemy (Acts 10:38, 1 John 3:8). Healing is also a part of

the name/unchanging character of God (*Jehovah—Rapha*, Exodus 15:26) and is now found in the name of Jesus (Acts 3:16), as an activity of the *same* Holy Spirit available to the church today (Luke 24:49, Acts 1:8, Acts 10:38). Such works are also as found throughout the whole of church history, albeit in pockets, through every century of the church.

Fundamentally, healing is also a part of the atonement (1 Corinthians 1:18). Jesus bore sickness and disease not only for those that He healed in first-century Palestine, but also 'the sicknesses of *us*'—this is the same Greek construction used in 1 Corinthians 15:3 for 'our sins', when Paul said, 'Christ died for the sins of *us*.' The healing of first-century Jesus was no more limited to those around Him then than is the forgiveness of Jesus. The Old Testament makes this clear also; Isaiah 53:4 has Jesus bearing and carrying (Hebrew verbs *nasa* and *sabal*) our sicknesses and pains, which are the same two verbs used in Isaiah 53:11–12 of sins and iniquities. Both verbs mean 'to bear vicariously or mediatorially'. This *is* the atonement. Evangelism is about supernatural forgiveness, deliverance and healing. Rebirth into the Kingdom of God is supernatural because the gospel is supernatural, because God is supernatural.

10.c) **Works**—Jesus quotes from the Jubilee passage of Isaiah 61 when He declares His Kingdom Party Manifesto in Luke 4 at the commencement of His public ministry. Jubilee, although without evidence of ever having been put into operation, was God's mandate for freedom from oppression and injustice, for the redistribution of wealth and the emancipation of slaves. His treatment of the outcasts of society (tax collectors, prostitutes, publicans, etc.) and His investment of women with dignity and self-worth (John 4:26, Mark 14:3–9, Matthew 28:1–10 etc.) in a sexist culture (Rabbinical quotations of the day concerning women include, 'Better to burn and bury the scriptures than teach them to a woman'; 'Better to be born dead than to be born a woman'; 'If you teach a woman the scriptures it is as bad as teaching her lechery'), were a part of this Jubilee manifesto of Kingdom good news.

In a team of twelve Jesus only appointed one functional position, and that was the treasurer (Judas!) to administer gifts to the poor (John 12:6). This emphasis on Kingdom works is perpetuated by Jesus' church, as one would expect (Acts 4:32–35, Acts 6:1–7, 1 Timothy 5, etc.).

Words, Wonders and Works are then the biblical constituent parts of the gospel. And this is why church is vital for effective evangelism, and is the only true base/root for biblical evangelism: Words evangelism doesn't need church, nor does Wonders evangelism, but effective Works evangelism can only be done thoroughly, consistently and credibly through the local body of Jesus Christ into a community. Holistic evangelism (*soterio*—salvation, wholeness, forgiveness) requires Words, Wonders, Works—in short, it requires church.

It is to this kind of church that the keys to the Kingdom of God are given in the only verse in the New Testament that links church and Kingdom (Matthew 16:18). If the keys of the *Kingdom* go to the *church*, and if evangelism is to be centred on the good news of the *Kingdom* (Matthew 9 and 10), then evangelism and church *must* come together. The government of the Kingdom of God rests on the shoulders of the Messiah (Isaiah 9:6); if Jesus is the *head* of the church (Colossians 1:18), then the government of His Kingdom rests on the shoulders of the body—on us, the church.

Kingdom, church and evangelism are parts of the same global, eternal plan of God, and evangelism will be both a priority and a consequence of a Kingdom church. Having a Kingdom theology like this enhances one's understanding of spiritual warfare and develops a very active, positive warfare theology; eschatology and radical evangelism are connected by the expectation that the latter will trigger the former, the bringing in of the Kingdom of God in fulness by a victorious though opposed church.

11. A further reason why evangelism must be church-based is because of *the effects on local church when evangelism* isn't *being done from that base.* Decline is the obvious factor here, although such decline may take longer than the lifespan of a generation, due to transfer growth. But ultimately and inevitably, without evangelism the death rate will overtake transfer growth rate. Transfer growth is never real growth and consequently a local church will die without evangelism. Imported missions will not suffice (though they may be *part* of an overall strategy) because church-based evangelism, and particularly church planting, has the facility of unlocking ministry and gifts potential in the local congregation.

So evangelism will demand local resources of manpower and finances organised into evangelism teams, public communication training schools, door-to-door teams, youth teams, housegroup evangelists, preaching evangelists, nurture group leaders and helpers, etc. Evangelism through church planting will demand leaders at every level: team leaders, praise and worship leaders, PA teams, administrators, housegroup leaders, a new Evangelism Team, etc.

Evangelism through the local church, and through local church planting, stimulates growth and demands a release of development at every level. Reactions to such demands and change can either be in fear, insecurity and stress, or in vision, faith and excitement. If the latter, then church, a living organism rather than a ticking clock, will be healthier for reproduction (Philemon, verse 6).

Evangelism from a local church base has a wonderful tendency to provide a focus for discipleship—many pastoral issues are sorted in the context of growth when introversion is denied. The New Testament knows no context for such discipleship other than the church, and as the Great Commission (Matthew 28:16–20) demands world evangelisation, in the context of the making of disciples, the link between church and evangelism is again established.

Evangelism through the local church necessitates a statement to church membership that *not* all of the jobs have already gone, that outlets will exist for training and development, that change will be the hallmark of maturity, that the dangers of stagnation, status quo, ritual, religion and tradition (all enemies of evangelism) will be avoided.

12. Finally, evangelism should be church-based because *the very root/heart of the Gospel, the empty cross of Jesus Christ, contains the very seeds of the church.* When Jesus hung on the Roman gibbet and the sinless became sin (1 Peter 3:18) and accursed to God (Galatians 3:13), He had not only individuals in heart and mind, but also church. Although she was not yet birthed, Jesus died *for* her and to establish her. Jesus had modelled embryonic church with His team of disciples, yet knew that without Calvary there would be no Pentecost, without sacrifice there would be no Holy Spirit outpouring. The Cross carries church right into the heart of the message *and* the means of the good news of Jesus Christ (Ephesians 5: 25–27).

Churches embarking upon this kind of radical evangelism will be fulfilling the roles used to describe church in the New Testament—they will be a *building* of living stones constantly being extended (1 Peter 2: 4–12). They will be a *body* of belonging, functioning, moving parts (1 Corinthians 12:12–27, Romans 12: 4–5). They will be a *bride* that is loving one another, God and themselves (Revelation 21:2 and 9, Luke 10:27) and they will be a *battalion* that is fighting, as all evangelism occurs on the interface beween two expansionist Kingdoms and is therefore warfare (Ephesians 6 :10–18, 2 Timothy 2: 3–4).

CHAPTER 7

GOD THE STRATEGIST

Once we determine that God desires to incarnationally communicate good news to all peoples, and given then that the first vital ingredient for radical New Testament evangelism is church (a root proposition which seems obvious, but clearly historically hasn't been the practice), then the second part of the process of effective evangelism is strategy.

The dangers of anthropomorphism are obvious—rather we have strategies because God is a strategist, and not vice versa. When humanity first fell away from God in Genesis 3 there is a clear indication of the redemption strategy of God in Jesus (Genesis 3:15). God's strategy for Noah, for the Ark, for Abraham, for Joseph, for Israel, all these litter the pages of the Old Testament. The strategy of a King who would be Messiah, yet also a Suffering Servant, runs through the prophetic book of Isaiah. The Old Testament is the back-drop strategy, the dictionary and the commentary for the New Covenant—God *is* a strategist.

Jesus the Strategist

Jesus came at a strategic time and place (God's choice and initiative—it could have been other) when the scene had been set (Old Testament, angels and Wise Men, John the Baptist). He came when the Roman road systems, common language, weights and measures, finances and government systems facilitated the quickest and easiest means of communication. And He came to a people under Roman rule to best demonstrate how to deal with injustice, racism and oppression (Matthew 5). Jesus had a strategy for training and developing His disciples:

- The pupil observes the teacher and asks questions.
- The teacher observes the pupil and poses questions.
- The pupils go out in pairs without the teacher.
- The teacher takes feedback from the pupils.

and for evangelism (Matthew 28:16–20, Acts 1:8, Ephesians 5:25–27).

Strategy in the Early Church

The early church, a part of that strategy, grew again through strategic evangelism. Such strategy was both God-initiated and church-initiated (Philip's meeting with the Ethiopian in Acts 8, or the apostolic appointing of deacons in Acts 6). Paul stated a part of his strategies in Romans 15:17–21, where he postulates evangelism done:

a) on virgin territory
b) in a saturation method
c) over a defined area (Jerusalem to southern Yugoslavia/Albania).

Paul's method of accomplishing this task reveals a further strategy of his: the planting of resource churches which would have the capacity and heart to replant other churches. He personally could never preach the gospel completely over an area of that size in the time available to him, but resource churches planted at strategic points of commerce, transport and occult activity could.

Paul's missionary journeys, so confusing with their proliferation of red lines on the maps at the back of many Bibles, do actually confirm Paul's strategy of getting the gospel to the Gentiles (Acts 11, 15). His orderly progress with Barnabas through Cyprus from

Salamis in the north to Pathos in the south (Acts 13: 4–6) indicates attention to strategy, as does his method of getting the gospel from Ephesus to Asia in Acts 19:8–10. God is a strategist. Jesus is a strategist. The church of Jesus is to be strategic.

CHAPTER 8

GOALS AND EVANGELISM

Strategies are biblical because God uses strategies to get His will done. Strategies require the setting of goals, and goals are vital to radical evangelism. God has a goal for evangelism (Matthew 24:14, 2 Peter 3:9). In Matthew 9:35 Jesus seems to have had a clear goal, which Josephus defines in his histories as seeking to reach approximately 15,000 people in 204 villages. If Jesus had goals to accomplish strategies, so should we. The strategy deals with how, the goal deals with results.

Results in evangelism are ultimately, of course, God's responsibility, and yet He is looking for active, positive, faith-filled participation (Matthew 11:12). The examples of goals in Scripture do away with the notion that goals and strategies are somehow unspiritual. Goals and strategies do not determine where or how the wind of the Holy Spirit blows, but they do help us to reset our sails. They do carry quite a high threat level however, because specifying a strategy and a goal means that failure will probably be both assessable and obvious, should it occur. It's easy to insist that we've hit our target if we draw it *after* we've fired; if we aim at nothing that's exactly what we hit.

However, pre-stated goals stop this kind of nonsense, and save us from super-spiritualising failure ('It must have been God's will; He's trying to teach us something; it's very difficult in this area; this is just a wilderness experience/dry patch/valley experience', etc.!!) Failure can either be a doorway to maturity or a trapdoor to obscurity, and super-spiritualising failure will mean the latter. There will be no lessons learned, no adjustments made, and no need for perseverance. Goals *can* be threatening and difficult to write, but the advantages are many:

1. Goals release *motivation* into individuals and churches. Church growth expert Peter Wagner says, 'If you get some goals which people believe are achievable and are worth achieving, people will lay down their lives for them.'

2 . Goals release *energy*. Wagner again: 'Some power is released through setting positive goals that otherwise remains dormant . . . it is a biblical principle that God seems to honour.'

3 . Goals take the emphasis off present problems and put it onto *future possibilities*. George Bernard Shaw said, 'You look at what is and say why; I look at what is not and say why not?'

4 . Goals establish a proper *sense of limit* to our call—establishing right boundaries rather than false barriers (Romans 12:3).

5. Goals facilitate *prayer* (James 4:2–3).

6. Goals lead to *'growth elbows'* (for example, church planting in the Philippines doubled between 1964 and 1974 because of goal setting). Yonggi Cho said, 'The number-one requirement for having real church growth is to set goals.'

Goals Are . . .

It is important that goals in evangelism are:

- specific
- personal as well as corporate
- measurable (in time and performance terms)

- achievable
- adjustable (e.g. Acts 16: 6–10)
- broken down into a series of steps.

If a goal is too big (and therefore produces lassitude or fear) it needs to be subdivided into primary and secondary goal sets. (How do you eat an elephant? A bite at a time!)

Goals learn *from* the past, but are not limited *by* it, getting us doing today what will favourably affect tomorrow.

It is necessary that goals be clear, uncomplicated and easily communicated, focusing existing resources whilst highlighting the need for further future resources and therefore leading to development, training, more prayer, more evangelism! (After all, the more people we have in our churches, the more resources we have!)

Finally, all goals should have a historical perspective—that is to say, they should have a short-, medium- and long-term range, and also have an inbuilt method of evaluation and assessment through feedback in order to determine whether we are on target.

Setting Goals

It is generally true that people don't have problems achieving goals, they only have problems setting them, which of course stops them achieving as much as they might. Goals are basically faith statements, so a prerequisite of setting them is to hear from God: 'Where to plant a church? When? Who to put on the team? On the leadership? Which estate to visit door to door? Which friends to invite to the evangelistic beer and skittles evening?' Hearing from God should be subject to checks and balances of the church; it is *together* that we understand the love of God for people (Ephesians 3:18) and have the mind of Christ (1 Corinthians 2:16). The following questions are also helpful when setting goals:

A. How *important* is the goal? (What am I investing

in? What will happen if I don't do it?)

B. How *urgent* is the goal? (refers more to the stress level and time demands)

C. Am I working from long- to medium- and from medium- to short-term goals, and not therefore just responding to need and to the immediate?

D. Can I forecast where we will be in ten years' time without change? What goals will get us to where we *want* to be?

E. How often must various tasks be done to accomplish the goals, and can someone else do them better/quicker?

F. Can I prioritise my goals, i.e. *leave* that which is low in urgency and importance, *delegate* that which is low in importance but high in urgency, *plan* that which is low in urgency but high in importance, and *do* that which is high in urgency and importance?

With God's heart and methods, with church, strategies and goals as the backdrop to radical evangelism, we now need to adopt a means of implementation and practical outworking. We need to take the principles above and apply them to the life of the local church. What follows is a framework within which specific situations can be slotted to help toward a strategy for growth.

Developing a Strategy for Growth

We shall posit five stages to developing a strategy for growth, each of which is vital to radical evangelism and which need to occur in the order of the following five chapters.

CHAPTER 9

COMMITMENT

1. Commitment to Growth

This is an issue of decision and will, needs to be made before plans are made, and must be wholehearted, for the cost of growth is second only to the cost of decline. This commitment to growth must be:

a) **From leadership**, thus avoiding the frustration of 'growth bottleneck'. The leadership—which biblically is plural, not 'one-man', and should reflect a variety of giftings (Ephesians 4:11–13)—must own the vision, and the wider leadership (e.g. housegroup leaders, youth group leaders, nurture group leaders, praise and worship leaders, administrators, etc.) must in turn represent this commitment to the church. It will not do for one leader or one small group of core leaders to own the vision without the wider leadership team both owning the vision, and communicating that vision to the church.

Church members must in turn be submitted to one another and to their leadership, and so if leadership isn't committed to growth (which is unbiblical) then church members cannot be submitted to those leaders, which will necessitate either a change of leadership or a change of church. Where leadership at every level is committed to growth, with clear goals before them, the first stage of developing a strategy for that growth is accomplished.

b) **From the whole church**. Throughout this *Perspective* on radical evangelism, for 'church-based evangelism' read '*whole*-church evangelism'. To be a disciple of Jesus is to be included in His Great Commission. All disciples are 'goers', so that in the context of evangelism, the question is not 'Should I go?' but rather 'Why shouldn't I go?' When Jesus first *called* His disciples He *commissioned* them immediately: 'Come and follow and become fishers of men.' When Peter stood and preached at Pentecost, he may have been the mouthpiece, but he stood 'with the eleven'—it was team and community evangelism right from the start (Acts 2:14). The Holy Spirit has been poured out for 'all flesh' (Joel 2:28–32, Acts 2:17) and He desires to fall in *dunamis* (dynamite) power on *all* Christians so that they *become* witnesses (Acts 1:8, as opposed to *doing* witnessing).

This evidence of the link between call and commission, of God's desire for the Holy Spirit to equip the *whole* church to do witnessing, is why the *euvangelistes* only appears three times in the New Testament; not because God isn't into evangelism, but because it's to be the work of the church (Ephesians 4:13), and so the word 'witness' (Greek *martureo*—martyr, indicating the cost and privilege of evangelism) appears much more frequently (63 times).

This word 'witness' is in a New Testament Jewish context where the witness must be first-hand and where hearsay evidence would not be accepted in a court of law (not unlike the English system). This is the style of witness that God requires of all of His disciples. Fuller Theological Seminary studies on church growth indicate that approximately 10% of any local church will be evangelists anointed by the Spirit of Jesus, and clearly we are *not* all evangelists, but equally clearly we *are* all witnesses. God's master plan for salvation involves all of the church to all of the world, not a kind of full-time/professional elite of evangelists.

2. Commitment to Communication

There is a danger that what the core team (plurality) of leadership spend days praying and strategising over is communicated to the wider leadership team in one two-hour session, and to the rest of the church in a

five-minute housegroup notice!   Leaders would do
well in such circumstances not to express surprise that
the whole church does not seem to have caught the
vision! Any strategy for growth must incorporate
multiple methods of communicating that vision.

The communication must be *creative* (i.e. weekends
of prayer and fasting, audio-visual aid presentations,
motivational preaching, training sessions, teaching
sessions, housegroup notices, church notices,
personal letters, phone calls, feedback forums,
members' meetings, etc.).

And it must also be *repetitive*. In Korea Yonggi Cho
estimates that it takes an individual six hearings of the
gospel before an intelligent response is made; in the UK
it is approximately seven times. We shouldn't be
surprised then that communication *about* the spreading
of that gospel also takes time and must be repetitive.
Juan Carlos Ortiz maintained that he would preach
on one subject repetitively until his church were
doing/living what he preached on. John Wimber had
the same experience of a year's preaching on healing
before anyone in his church actually was healed.

The strategy for evangelism will include alterations
to the preaching/teaching timetable, to the homegroup
study plan of the local church, not only until the vision
can be written down by every church member in a two-
minute exercise in any such forum, but also until the
vision has been owned by all church members and not
just understood by them.

3. Commitment to Change

Many churches have become institutions of religion
rather than organisms of life. Their methods of
worship are designed to bring comfort and security to
the worshipper instead of pleasure to God. Their
traditions and ceremonies speak of a God who is
remote and irrelevant, their vestments speak of
authority and institutionalism. Even when the wind
of the Holy Spirit of change blows, all too quickly
church can settle back into repetitive chorus singing,

some charismatic churches merely switching a tongue sandwich for a hymn sandwich!

Yet in the Kingdom of God constant change is here to stay. Only God is Holy. Only His character doesn't change. His methods certainly do. A mark of maturity is the ability not only to change but to embrace positive change, and also to cope with negative change.

Evangelism has the capacity to make church evaluate everything it does from an outsider mentality, assessing how 'seeker sensitive' we are and how effective our 'seeker targeting' is. The commitment to evangelism is a commitment to change. The nature of our *youth work* may change. The make-up of our *leadership teams* may change. Our *meetings* will change to be more meaningful, and perhaps our *style of public communication* also. The way *praise and worship* are led/explained may need adjustment. The *structures* of our church may be too unwieldy or parochial.

My own church changed its leadership model from all local leaders being elders to a smaller oversight, with more localised congregational leaders, and subsequently experienced a very fast 'growth elbow' as a better grasp of overall vision, and a quicker ability to respond to local evangelistic and pastoral situations, were thus effected.

Church diaries will change, adding guest meetings here, dropping in-house church celebrations for evangelistic cabarets there, freeing one housegroup evening per month for friendship evangelism, running monthly streetwork in the town centre, etc. The *priorities on our agendas* will shift—from business to warfare, from maintenance to outreach, from roof repairs to funding an Evangelistic Team. Make no mistake—that to which we give priority will be that to which those whom we are leading also give priority.

The church *name* itself may need to change; many New Churches call themselves Christian Fellowships, but the word Fellowship smacks of introversion, exclusivity and is rather sect-like. A much better phrase would be Community Church, both of which words say something about who we are and are something which the average non-Christian can understand. Appending a place-name to the front of Community Church (e.g. Chichester Community Church) may not be the most helpful, as the vision of the local church may expand beyond the local town, particularly as church planting gets under way. Such a name would therefore then be limiting and a more neutral name may be more appropriate. (Consequently my own church on the south coast is now called Revelation—A Church in your Community. This is because we currently have congregations in six different towns, with six different identities, although we remain the one church.)

CHAPTER 10

DEVELOPMENT

After commitment in the areas outlined in the last chapter, the second stage in devising a strategy for growth is *development*. Development is the only difference between reality and aspiration. Disciples are made, they are not born. A church's ability to create effective witnesses, and subsequently to do effective witnessing, will depend upon that church's investment in development, which is of course the role of the evangelist.

Principles of Development

There are a number of important principles in developing and releasing evangelistic ministry into the life of local church:

1. Selection of the right personnel (Matthew 4:18)—after Holy Spirit-led prayer and fasting, looking through church lists, being wary of people blindness and yet avoiding taking on people who are merely in pastoral 'holes'—note that Jesus spent time with Peter, James and John as well as with Judas! The key points here are to look for teachability, availability, faithfulness, fruitfulness, and above all, that people have a servant heart.

2. Demonstration by example (Matthew 4:23). Schweitzer said, 'Example is not the best means of leadership, it's the *only* means.' The demonstration should include the importance of identity before function, and the principle and practice of service in both the general sphere and in the specific areas of gifting. (Anyone and everyone should be prepared to be putting the chairs out at evangelistic meetings, but not everyone will be doing the evangelistic preaching.)

3. Instruction (Matthew 5—7)—into character, as well as into gifting, to impart skills and not merely to give answers. We are looking to train people who realise not only what works, but also *why* things work, and therefore can develop the ability to conceptualise concerning skills, can expand their own creative material, and can teach others. This development is intrinsic and not extrinsic, or extraneous. Such instruction is aimed at head, heart *and* will, and is best done as Jesus did it—have the learner ('disciple': one who learns, keeps a discipline) with the trainer (Mark 3:14), encourage questions (Matthew 18:1–4), rebuke and confront in love where necessary (Matthew 19:14).

4. Impartation (Matthew 10)—where the trainer reproduces who and what he is, whilst avoiding building over-exclusive relationships (I can train well in some areas within the 'window' of my gifting, but not so well in others, hence team ministry) and allowing the disciple to pay the price of failure in order later to cope with the price of success.

5. Delegation (Matthew 28:16–20). The Great Commission is a supreme act of delegation, giving decision-making power to others (and passing on the good jobs as well as the bad ones!) in an environment of trust and safety, where failure is allowed, experimentation encouraged and change embraced. *Kakahaphiaphobia* is the fear of failure and the enemy of delegation, whereas failure can lead to a redemptive positive learning experience. Delegation means that if things go well the learners get the credit, if badly then the trainer carries the responsibility and the blame! In the short term delegation doesn't work (rather like the cross of Jesus Christ) and it takes longer, often with less success. But in the long term it is a vital part of training and development. Remember, too, that it is irresponsible to train and develop individuals and then to deny them access to opportunities for action and responsibility. That kind of information leads not to transformation, but to frustration in individuals' lives.

Levels of Development

There are three levels on which church must be developed to produce growth and healthy evangelism, so that the church becomes evangelistic, rather than merely doing evangelistic events. These are:

1. the whole church (see Jesus' relationship with the 70 in Luke 10 and with the 120 and the 500);
2. the 'able keenies' (see Jesus and the twelve in Luke 9);
3. the anointed individuals (see Jesus and the three in Mark 9:2, and Jesus and the one in John 21:22).

The three groupings will determine the content and the style of the developmental approach.

1. Whole church
Development of the whole church should include *motivation* and *envisioning* (Proverbs 29:18), *teaching* which establishes a biblical base, therefore increasing head knowledge and understanding (Hosea 4:6), and also *training*, which is the application of theory to practice. This is a discipleship model. A minimum from my perspective would include six monthly joint housegroup training sessions with homework set after each two-hour session. These meetings would be centred around subjects covering:

- who does evangelism
- whom we evangelise—friendship evangelism
- why we evangelise
- what stops us
- what the gospel is

- whose territory we evangelise on—spiritual warfare
- how we witness—covering communication, apologetics
- leading someone to Christ
- using your testimony.

These teaching sessions aimed at the whole church would also seek to teach the church to appreciate the nature of evangelism in order to combat long-term disillusionment and apathy.

Evangelism is holistic—one cannot do evangelism without success somewhere (Isaiah 55:11). Not all of evangelism is about reaping, some is about sowing, broadcasting seed. Every encounter with people about God will move them along a scale in their knowledge of God and this scale was best identified by Christian sociologist Dr Engel, ranging from no knowledge/ belief in God (from point 0; only 9% of the UK adult population are atheist) to salvation (point 10). Salvation is a process, and points 0 to 6 on the Engel scale of relationship to God are about sowing, often based on works of the gospel. Points 7 to 10 are about reaping, often based on wonders and words; but it is *all* about evangelism, 0 to 10! Much reaping with little sowing leads to difficulties of new convert integration (friendship evangelism works best of all; 80% of Christians are converted through it!)

Such teaching on the wider picture of what constitutes evangelism and how we measure its success rating will help the church identify what are its hard and soft areas (geographically and by people networks) and therefore which strategies to adopt over what period of time (i.e. short-, medium- or long-term?)

Such training meetings should incorporate both teaching and training, but really ought to come after up to three motivational preaching sessions on evangelism to the whole church.

If such training is embarked upon then either the local church evangelist must be involved, or in their absence, a specialist must be drawn in from the church's network of individual friendships and apostolic relationships. This is essential, since the specialist (in this case the evangelist) will always spot other specialists in their field within the church (those 10% referred to earlier), even when they are still in the embryonic 'rough diamond' state. The evangelist will tend not to have 'people blindness', which can lock church leadership into only seeing their people's past problems and pastoral failings (due to familiarity), rather than seeing their potential in God.

2. 'Able keenies'
Whole church development along these lines will give access and opportunity to the evangelist to spot evangelistic talent, and for the leaders then to recruit that talent by invitation, perhaps onto an Evangelism Team. There is then room for more specific teaching/training on particular areas of evangelism relevant to the church's strategy, pitched at this group of 'able keenies'! For example, such teaching and training might incorporate door-to-door work and strategy, streetwork, schools work, youth club work, pub evangelism, questionnaire work, detached youth work, events evangelism, guest meetings, etc.

3. Anointed individuals
It is from this group of 'able keenies' that the anointed individuals will appear, and the need for sending trainees out from the church may emerge, to make good use of training projects (which essentially ought to be church-based) like TIE Teams (Training in Evangelism Teams, a Pioneer Team project—details available from the Pioneer Office whose address is on page 2).

So, development involves releasing (or alternatively, if necessary, bringing in) the *specialist/evangelist*; it involves motivating, teaching and training *the whole church*, identifying, teaching and training *the keenies*, and identifying, teaching and training (on a discipleship model) *anointed individuals* within the context of local church where possible, but being prepared to release those individuals to the wider church scene where necessary. This is the second stage of determining a strategy for growth.

CHAPTER 11

RESEARCH AND REVELATION

When King David was assessing the strength of Israel and preparing his people for warfare (which is partly what evangelism is all about) he leaned heavily on his strategists, the men of Issachar, who understood the times and acted and advised accordingly (1 Chronicles 12:32). Research is a necessary part of radical evangelism and will set and hone strategies and goals. Research must go hand in hand with revelation as the third stage, so that the strategy for growth is determined by both head and heart. Scripture teaches that for lack of both knowledge and vision the people of God perish and lose their sense of direction and destiny (Hosea 4:6, Proverbs 29:18).

Both research and revelation are methods employed by Jesus in His extension of God's Kingdom. In Luke 13:12, where it would seem natural to be praying for physical healing, Jesus is rebuking a spirit of infirmity (going for root causes and not for fruit or symptoms), identified, one presumes, through the discernment of spirits, which is of course a revelation gift. Yet in Mark 9:21 Jesus chooses to ask a pertinent question of the afflicted child's father—this root is determined more by research than by revelation.

Both research and revelation need to be used to assess the following areas important to developing the strategy for growth:

1. People

Who are the people God has given to you to evangelise? Is it everyone in a given area? If so, what area? What size of population? What distribution of age range? What type of housing? Where do they work/shop/socialise? If not everyone, then which particular people group? The young? The old? The unemployed? The rich? Where are they and what do they do?

2. Boundaries

Are there clear geographical boundaries within which to work? A river? A major road? A railway line? A housing estate? A town? (For example, London is huge, yet made up of a series of town/village mentalities, which people are loathe to cross.) Is the boundary between council and private housing? Demography is much affected by geography.

3. Needs

What are the needs of the people and area that you have identified in (1) and (2) above? Felt need is a good place to start in evangelism—it is a springboard for communication and a platform for serving communities.

A community survey (door-to-door) is a helpful pointer towards people's perceived needs in an area. Do they need more shops? A launderette? Are there lonely OAPs? Do they need coffee mornings? What about youth work? Are there litter problems? Such information provides a useful opportunity for the local church to contact (and re-contact with survey results) people on their doorsteps, to begin to provide social action to alleviate felt need (a part of the gospel) and to be involved, for example, politically, in order to see justice brought to such areas of deprivation (also a part of the gospel).

Such survey statistics and social action will also

gain the church a credible profile through the local media. It is often from such a detailed survey that information will be built up to help answer the questions posed in (1) and (2) above. More people groups will be thus identified, popular pubs will be spotted (including those giving opportunities for under-age drinking), youth clubs and organisations listed (Scouts, Cubs, Beavers, Guides, etc.). Venues will be confirmed for doing detached youth work (e.g. outside local pubs, clubs, fish and chip shops, video stores, off-licences, and on particular street corners and parks), schools can be targeted, presentation streetwork locations identified, parades of shops assessed for questionnaire streetwork, numbers of houses in an area noted, major employers and factories, OAP homes and hospitals included into the strategy for evangelism, etc.

4. Spiritual Warfare

One very good aim of local church-based evangelism is for that church to become the dominant spiritual force in its area. That aim will automatically bring about spiritual warfare, which is an integral part of evangelism, as both God's and Satan's kingdoms are expansionist, each seeking to be dominant over the lives of individuals, churches, villages, towns, cities, counties, nations, continents and indeed the world. Spiritual warfare goes on all the time, everywhere, at every level. Behind each individual is a system, each system is built on values and behind those values lie principalities and powers, just as behind each believer in Christ is the church, built on Scripture, behind which is the Holy Spirit.

Research and revelation will help to determine the dominant negative spiritual forces behind individual lives, towns, areas, etc. (As a network of local churches, Pioneer has a clear perspective on territorial spirits and a credible theology behind that, backed up by the experience of successful evangelism, which has been based upon effectively waged territorial spiritual warfare. This is theology meeting experience.) Prayer walks can produce lists of words of knowledge over specific houses, and visions of spiritual forces over streets, etc. Historical research will betray trends in an area—as a local church in Bognor Regis, for example, we traced the failure of churches in the area to a curse placed on those churches by a superstitious and bitter seamen's mission in the last century. The town was birthed in failure and bankruptcy by Sir Richard Hotham, and indecision and political impotence from its very roots is still dogging local councils. The purported words of King George VI on his deathbed (not the reported 'How goes it with the Empire?' but rather, in bitter despair against his place of convalescence, 'Bugger Bognor') have added to the scenario of Bognor as the butt of many of the nation's jokes, and its name doesn't help!

Much of this is self-imposed negative prophecy: curses need to be broken; political influence needs to be wielded for good; commerce needs to be practised with integrity; isolation needs to be broken from the lives of many retired people in the area; futility and despair needs to be combated in the lives of many homeless young people, and a dignity and self-worth must be restored through the power of the gospel to the lives of many of the individuals of Bognor.

When my home church, Revelation, first planted into Bognor in September 1986, the town had a very bad reputation with the local police for violence. At that time the CID force in the town was some eighteen strong, out of all proportion to the rest of West Sussex. Anyone arrested would be at least as likely to fight the arresting officer as to come quietly. Having identified this trend (police statistics, a converted policeman, and a close eye on the local press all helped) the church began to wage warfare into this scenario through prayer and fasting, praise and worship, and now, six years later, the town is notably quieter; the CID force has been reduced to six, and the reputation of Bognor Regis amongst the police is much restored.

Helpful starting places to find such information are the local press and local library, parish records, historical societies, talking with OAPs, council records, the corner shop notice board, in local pubs, and by mid-1992 the latest National Census statistics on population and demography will be released.

Finally, revelation and research accrued over these four areas must be recorded on file, computer and maps; we need to be accountable to God and to our area for the words of knowledge, visions and prophecies received, and for our surveys undertaken.

CHAPTER 12

ACTION—INTERNAL

So far a strategy for growth has progressed from a *commitment* to growth (affecting leadership and the whole church, and effecting communication and change) through *development* (across whole church, keen activists and anointed individuals) to *research and revelation* (of people, needs, geography, and spiritual backdrop). *Action* is the next part of the process.

Action arising from a strategy for growth will be both internal (to the church) and external (to the community). In this chapter, we shall consider internal action as it affects five areas of church life.

1. Leadership

It is likely that the local church leadership team will need to be wider, along the lines of Ephesians 4:11–13. Ideally local church evangelists will be brought alongside of or onto the core leadership team of the church (elders, oversight, diaconate, PCC, whatever), where their heart, thinking, strategies and perspectives can be harnessed and released. Many local church leadership teams are still pastoral in orientation and maintenance-minded and this must be changed.

Where the local church seems not to have such an anointed evangelist then *relational* links, which are *apostolic* (i.e. more than friendship/advice, but rather recognising apostolic function, fathering, moral and doctrinal input, leadership appointment and church planting oversight) must bring in such a ministry at this level, until it can reproduce itself within the church and the church's leadership.

It is not necessary to have an evangelist as the 'bottom line', 'first among equals' leader of such a team, although sometimes that will be appropriate. Many times that kind of responsibility and function will lock the evangelist up into practical and pastoral detail that may blunt their gifting. Where such lock-up occurs it will not only be unhelpful to the evangelist, but it will also be unhelpful to the local church! But it is vital that the evangelist has access to core leadership to help develop evangelistic strategy.

2. Meetings

Meetings may also need to be changed to make them more accessible to non-Christians. The centrality and suitability of the premises are important—a Baptist church in a town in the south of England recently had the only unlisted cinema in that town demolished in order to make way for their new church building, against much protest from local residents, making access to that new church for most of the residents most unlikely and unwanted! Their social accessibility is more important than their decor (i.e. I know of several inner-city church plants meeting in local pubs). Neutrality of premises is a factor in favour of evangelism, rather than any kind of ecclesiastical building.

The capacity of the building is important—church growth studies indicate that when 80% of capacity is reached a 'comfort factor' creeps in inhibiting further growth; 60% of capacity is about right—much smaller and the 'insignificance factor' applies, making the group feel smaller than it is. Churches grow quickest between 100 and 150, with the average size of a UK church now being 127, so a further change which will encourage growth would be the apostolic formation of multiple, community-relating congregational plants—one church, shared resources, many congregations. (Avoid the trap of local pastors or evangelists trying to plant churches without full Ephesians 4 team input.) Such congregations can be set up each time an already established congregation reaches the figure of about 150. The only exception to this would be when there is one mother church which is planting several times and that base probably needs to be more like 200 strong.

A good number to start a plant with is about 30, headed by a strong leadership team, 'bottom-lined' by a key 'breakthrough' person. (This should be someone with a clear understanding of church and the Kingdom of God; a ready conceptual grasp of practical theology; a charismatic personality in terms of church and meeting leadership. It should be someone who will draw people around themselves through their leadership giftings, and one who is clearly anointed of God to make things happen around them, with a clear evangelistic edge, although not necessarily themselves an evangelist.)

Ideally the meetings must change to encompass these growth-favourable numbers, and they must be seeker-sensitive, with explained worship and gifts of the Holy Spirit, gospel content threaded throughout, the opportunity for response to the gospel, and the avoidance of 'in jokes'. Visitors should be welcomed with applause, free publicity about the church and invitations to social meals, etc. No one part of the meeting should take too long (including the talk!), and there should be a sensitive approach to prayer groups, communion, collections, etc. Consistency of meeting times and place is also helpful in gaining profile and visitors.

3. Structures

Structures may also need to change. Is the youth group only catering for Christian youth? Are there nurture groups in place, and 'Only Looking' groups? Any evangelism strategy must put into place the means of church-based discipling, to make followers out of converts. A one-to-one plus small nurture group system outlining the basics of the faith (in our church called a 'Foundation Course' and running for ten weeks), plus a basic church outline (in our church called 'Church and You', running for five weeks), leading on into homegroups, is essential. We now keep 70% of our converts, where once we lost 70%.

Foundation Courses require our best leaders, with pastoral trainees—the church must strategise and structure for growth before receiving it. How does a new convert become part of the church membership? Are church expectations and definitions spelled out in the current structure somewhere? Are homegroups too introverted? Is there an Evangelism Team/Welcome Team? (In our own church we'd call the latter Teddy Bears!) Is there a Visitation Team? How and when and where do we train and develop our people?

All these questions will mitigate structural change to facilitate a strategy for growth. For example, home-groups that have previously existed for pastoral support only will probably need a shake-up of personnel. They will need defining along geographical membership lines to help the group 'own' an area, a specific number of doors to visit, streets to prayer-walk, etc. An evangelist will need to be put alongside the pastoral leader in a leadership capacity, and in addition at least one representative of the Evangelism Team should be a member of each homegroup.

It may be that commitment to an Evangelism Team means a release from commitment to membership of a homegroup, and that the Evangelism Team are found a pastoral support system elsewhere. Special evangelistic homegroup events may need to combine key couples and individuals *across* homegroups who are good at friendship evangelism, and there may now need to be homegroup evangelistic budgets drawn up by their leadership, publicity printed, venues and artists booked, etc. All of these things will have implications upon the administrative and financial structures of the church.

4. Prayer

Prayer structures are a further internal adjustment that

will be affected by developing a strategy for growth. Multiple means of praying evangelism into the church can be found. For example, each homegroup can spend fifteen minutes at the start of each of its weekly meetings praying in triplets for three named non-Christian friends. The group can go on bi-monthly prayer walks and drives around its geographical area, whilst the church overall can organise prayer marches (March for Jesus style).

Prayer-walking the boundaries of the area that God has given to that church, pulling together prayer concerts (using video, slides, maps, prayer boards, etc.) and half-nights and weekends of prayer and fasting are all possibilities. The Evangelism Team or evangelist can feed regular prayer information into the life of the church prayer meeting. Prayer in groups and all together can be prioritised in the church's main meetings. Telephone prayer chains, prayer letters, schools of intercessors, etc., are other ways of raising prayer profile, linked specifically to evangelism, across the whole church. If the whole church is to be talking to people about God, then the whole church should be talking to God about people.

5. Finance

A final but important aspect of internal action is finance. Jesus said, 'Where your treasure is, there your heart will be also,' and the reverse is also true (Matthew 6:21)! Evangelism will cost in terms of time, faith, energy and money. Any strategy for growth will need to be resourced by the booking of venues, use of publicity, generous funding of specialists (evangelists, evangelistic musicians, drama teams, etc.), provision of food and drink at cabarets, lights, PA, tracts and Bibles, props, clip boards and pens, name badges, administrative back-up (counselling forms, computer data-base, stationery, phone and fax, files, etc.). Ideally any local church should be looking to budget 45% of its gross income on evangelism, 45% on maintenance, and 10% to be given outside the local area. Similarly the release of 'full-time' personnel should reflect that balance, giving at least equal priority to putting evangelists out full-time as to putting out pastors, teachers, administrators, etc.

CHAPTER 13

ACTION—EXTERNAL

1. Friendship Evangelism

The more people are involved in living evangelistic lifestyles and evangelistic activity, the more non-Christians will be contacted and the more conversions will be professed, the more disciples will be made, the more churches will be planted, and so the cycle continues. Whole-church evangelism is best based on friendship evangelism—the 80% statistic quoted earlier breaks down as follows: in a survey conducted amongst 10,000 Christians, 1% of them were converted through crusades, 1% through visitation, 1% through a period of personal crisis, 3% through cold church contact (wandering into a church meeting), 3% through specific events, 5% through Sunday School, 6% as a result of the work of a church leader, and 80% through friendship evangelism! 'There is only one way not to be won over by love, and that is to flee from it' (Napoleon Bonaparte). This is the Jesus method, the Son of God who is a *friend* of sinners' (Luke 15:1–2).

There are excellent biblical precedents for friend-ship evangelism, working as it does across the networks or people groups (those *te ethne* again—all nations/people groups/ethnic groups of Matthew 28:16–20) that everyone has. These networks can be categorised as:

- family
- neighbours
- church fringe
- work contacts
- social contacts.

The Bible gives many instances of these networks being worked for the gospel (e.g. John 1:40–50, Luke 5:17–32, John 9:1–41, John 4:28–39, Mark 1:29–31, Mark 2:3, Mark 7:25, Mark 8:22, Mark 9:17, Mark 10:13, Mark 14:3, etc.). Teaching can activate the whole church to name at least one individual per network (that will give us five names per church member), to evaluate and develop these friendships, to pray into them, to see them converted. This is the bedrock of any strategy for growth.

Successful friendship evangelism can take a lot of time and effort and will necessitate repetitive teaching and training to get it up and running and to keep the evangelistic edge on it, but the effort is worthwhile. It is upon friendship evangelism that successful events evangelism is built—not either/or, but both/and.

It is worth noting too that new converts have the best and widest networks in which to 'fish'; we must avoid both extremes—either of so pastoring and teaching the new convert and thus locking them into church life to the detriment of their non-Christian contacts, or alternatively of putting them under such pressure to witness to their new-found faith, before they've had the chance to ask their own questions and discover their own identity in Christ, that they eventually cave in under that pressure.

2. Events Evangelism

Starting with the action point of friendship evangelism helps us get events evangelism into a helpful perspective. Evangelistic events are that part of the strategy for growth which is designed to service the friendship evangelism already going on among (*all*) church members, in order to best serve those church members with appropriate evangelistic events.

The members should be polled as to what type of event they would like to invite their non-Christian friends to. An evangelistic rock concert might attract a people group made up of teenagers, but might do little for middle-aged doctors, solicitors and accountants. The best strategy is to develop a range of evangelistic events of differing styles.

This alone is insufficient for an events strategy, however. In addition to this range of *style*, the events should differ in the *amount of gospel content*, ranging from the purely social to the full-blown gospel presentation with appeal. Thus an evangelistic event in January which is a rock concert might have very little gospel content, but by December that evangelistic event might be a rock concert with gospel preaching and appeal. The sliding scale of content can work over the course of one year or much longer.

My own church homegroups have held summertime low-key evangelistic events for three years running, yet only this coming (fourth) summer are they ready to reap. One of our church plants has spent a year building fringe contacts and developing profile into the community, and now this next year is going higher profile, to reap some of that fringe. The scale must be determined by an evaluation of the strength of relationships involved. (Don't try to drive a 10-ton gospel message over a 5-ton relational bridge!)

Another important factor in assessing the scale is the hardness of the area (one of our council estates responds quickly to neighbourly-based coffee mornings, one very middle-class area responds better to charitable events). Thus the expected short-, medium- or long-term approach can be estimated. Some areas will take five years to crack, some one year, etc.

Instead of spreading the gospel content across a certain time period like a year or five years, it is possible to alternate high gospel content with low from one evangelistic event to another. This is because there will always be some people ready to be reaped into the Kingdom. Some events will also have their 'seasons of success'—so for a little while my own church used evangelistic cabarets very successfully, but latterly we have concentrated more on playschemes and Family Fundays. Change and creativity are highlights of events evangelism, as is the key concept that each people group, and probably each geographical area, will require a different set of sliding-scale evangelistic events.

3. Seasonal Evangelism

Events can often be linked to key times of the year for any local community. I suggest that any strategy for growth needs to take account of at least seven such times and to work a year's evangelistic programme accordingly.

New Year provides a good time for events like a disco. Valentine's Day might prompt a Valentine's Ball or Barn Dance. Easter is a good time for guest and healing meetings. Summertime lends itself very well to detached youth work, to a Midsummer's Day Ball, It's-a-Knockout, Family Funday, Treasure Hunt, playschemes, etc. Hallowe'en might suggest an alternative buffet, a Saints and Sinners Fancy Dress Party, a non-Fancy Dress Party, whilst Bonfire Night is a good opportunity for a bonfire with food and games, and Christmas, of course, lends itself well to pantomimes, guest meetings, streetwork with free mince pies, door-to-door carol singing with a gospel presentation, etc.

There are many other imaginative events that can be added to such a framework, and which can be run across the whole church or by homegroups (e.g. Pub Trivia, Beer and Skittles, Pimms & Pancakes, Coffee and Gateaux, Cheese and Wine, Games Marathon Evening, Make-up Evening, Coffee Morning, Beach Bar-B-Q, Drinks and Nibbles, etc.)

4. Cold-Contact Evangelism — Visitation Progammes

Given that friendship evangelism does fail in respect of saturation evangelism (we will never know everyone in an area!), a growth strategy must also incorporate a high level of cold-contact evangelism. Healing Meetings, 'Religious Festival' guest meetings like

Christmas and Easter, Kids' Clubs, Fundays, all lend themselves well to attracting such cold contacts and should be included in the strategy accordingly. Other points of contact must be found so that the principle of multiple contacting can come alongside saturation evangelism (i.e. little Johnnie is seen in his Cub group, his sister at her school, both of them and their mother on the streets, and father through door-to-door contacting, the whole family at a Family Funday, and the family is saved at a subsequent church guest meeting—this is an actual case study).

So the strategy for growth will include a comprehensive door-to-door visitation programme, where the aim is to accrue information, to build relationships and friendships across the doorstep as quickly as possible, to find valid responses for return visits and to see people saved. If people in the UK tend to respond to the gospel on the seventh time of hearing, then our door-to-door strategy should include a revisiting tactic. This might run along the following lines:

VISIT 1   Community Survey

VISIT 2   Results Report

VISIT 3   Invitation to events designed to alleviate felt community needs discovered through Visit 1 and Visit 2.

VISIT 4   Attitudes Survey on Beliefs.

VISIT 5   Results Report.

VISIT 6   Offers of Prayer/Social Action. (A church in Wigan, having targeted a specific area, pushed Prayer Request Cards through the doors, collected them, prayed over them, and then re-visited and noted a 10% response from the door-to-door work.)

VISIT 7   On-going leaflet/invitation visit or drop.

I would incorporate into this strategy a progressive leaflet drop (for example, three small handbills which get progressively clearer in their message) between Visits 3 and 4.

Any such scheme must have a good data-base; who

has been visited by whom, and with what results? What literature was given, what impressions/words of knowledge received, who was out, who wants further literature/contact/return visits, etc.? This data-base should be constantly monitored by the door-to-door team and 'hot' contacts worked upon, invited to meetings, etc.

The best way of carrying out this kind of visitation is to have it spearheaded by a team of trained church members, and supplemented by all homegroup members (around the area of that homegroup, which ideally has geographically constituted membership) through 'waves of evangelism'. This means that each homegroup goes out on the doors (in pairs) approximately two evenings per week for two weeks every four months. Light evenings lend themselves to survey and questionnaire work, darker evenings to leaflet drops. Each wave of evangelism can carry its own pre-action training, as outlined earlier.

On average the take-up from door-to-door work is only 1%, but with a good prayer, warfare and events strategy linked in, I have seen that rise to 17%, and of course door-to-door work also gives profile to the local church and is a powerful statement of intent to principalities and powers in an area, as well as a useful training and motivational tool for the Christians.

5. Streetwork

Streetwork is another means of maximising cold-contact evangelism and of giving profile to local church. A strategy for streetwork should include questionnaire streetwork (e.g. outside a shopping parade, by a railway station, etc.), presentation streetwork (drama, busking, preaching, testimonies, etc., in a shopping mall or precinct), and detached youth work (outside the local youth club/pub, video shop, take-away, park, amusement arcade, etc.), and can involve working bus or bank queues with free shoe-shining service or sampling different kinds of Coke, etc.

Imagination, creativity and fun are the hallmarks of good streetwork, which is best done by a trained team of church members with other church members as 'rent-a-crowd'! If every homegroup has an evangelist as well as a pastor in leadership, plus an Evangelism Team representative as suggested earlier, then it shouldn't be too difficult to encourage other members of that homegroup to join in the streetwork. One Saturday per month is a good target for regular streetwork into one defined area, with more during special events like playscheme weeks, etc.

6. Specialist Teams

By combining whole-church evangelism with specialist teams, the best of both worlds is achieved in a strategy for growth; mass mobilisation and manpower, plus expert breakthrough personnel. These teams can be targeted at specific people groups and should ideally cover youth (the optimum age for salvation in the UK is 14 years and 9 months), through detached youth work, schools, existing clubs in the church and outside it. In addition a Visitation Team should aim specifically at door-to-door work. A Streetwork Team should be covering presentation and questionnaire streetwork. A 'Teddy Bear' Team can cover guest meetings. Social Action Teams can cover community involvement and the local political scene.

If manpower isn't available across all these groups, then the development of one Evangelism Team to target these groups would be vital. Such an Evangelism Team should be recruited by personal invitation of the leadership, with clearly defined expectations and criteria (for example, one evening per week on the doors, one Saturday per month on the streets, and regular input into guest meetings, homegroup strategy formation, church prayer meetings, etc.). It will need a leader (an evangelist) and a deputy leader (also an evangelist) and should determine its own training course, bringing in specialists as necessary for specialised training on streetwork, door-to-door work, running evangelistic events, signs and wonders in evangelism, spiritual warfare, voice projection, etc.).

Such a team will also need either its own administrative gifting or access to the church's administration base (e.g. for follow-up, venue booking and publicity purposes) and should ideally have its own praise and worship leader and drama co-ordinator. The numbers in such an Evangelism Team should approximate to 10% of the membership of the church, in order for that team to be healthy and sufficiently representative of the life of that local church. Setting up such a team or teams is a part of a growth strategy.

7. 'Kick-Start'

Finally, 'kick-starts' such as major missions or taking a Pioneer short-term TIE Team, or a Pioneer church-planting Hit Squad, over the summer can give a really powerful, fast and dynamic impetus to local church evangelism, particularly when that church is involved in church planting. Such kick-starts should also be considered as essential to this action outline of a developed strategy for growth.

CHAPTER 14

ASSESSMENT AND PERSISTENCE

These are the final aspects of a strategy for growth. Each part of the strategy needs to be assessed and have clear goals by which success and failure can be measured; each must have its own clear criteria and parameters—commitment levels, leadership and whole-church involvement, communication and vision, flexibility for change, development and training, research and revelation, internal and external action.

Assessment accesses adjustment. When failure occurs (some parts of the strategy will work better than others, some parts won't apparently work at all), there is then the opportunity for such adjustment.

Assessment balanced by persistence will help answer questions like, 'When do we move onto the doors on a new street or estate? When do we change from evangelistic concerts to cabarets? How soon can we expect to see a convert from our streetwork? How many converts are in church membership three or six or twelve months after conversion?'

Listed on the next page are a set of questions which will help a church leadership and its members towards establishing a strategy for growth. I am indebted to Steve Clifford of the Pioneer Team and the leadership of TIE Teams and of the Pioneer church in Cobham for their use, and suggest that you use them as a kind of checklist. If we learn to ask the right questions, then hopefully we are on the right route to finding the right answers!

1. What's your area?
2. What's the social make-up of your area?
3. What's the geographical distribution of your area?
4. What's the social make-up of the church?
5. What's the geographical distribution of the church?
6. What's the age distribution of the church?
7. What are the social needs of the area?
8. What contact do church members have with non-Christians? (Is this encouraged or discouraged?)
9. What evangelism is going on at present in the church?
10. What are the resources available for evangelism?
    (a) Money? (b) People? Are they enough?
11. What skills do church members need to acquire in order to be more effective in evangelism? How can you provide them with these skills?
12. Do we have any individuals in the church with specific evangelistic skills, whom we need to encourage and recognise?
13. What are other churches in the area doing in evangelism?
14. How is the church perceived in the area? Can this be changed?
15. Are there individuals in the church with key roles in the community who can be supported (e.g. doctors, teachers, local councillors, youth workers, social workers, etc.)?
16. What type of event would the church members like to invite their friends/neighbours/workmates/family along to?
17. How does the church follow up new Christians? Does it work?
18. Does the church have a fringe which can be evangelised?
19. How would church meetings be perceived by a newcomer? Would they be welcomed? Would

they understand what was going on? Would they find out how to get further involved? Would they be invited back afterwards?

20. How do people find out about our church? Would they be able to get to one of our meetings if they wanted to? Are our meetings in the best place?
21. Do we have any church literature? Is it good?
22. Are there opportunities in local schools/ youth clubs? Do we have young people who can be encouraged to reach their friends?
23. Should we be considering church planting?
24. Are there any dominant spiritual holds on the area, or the people in the area, which need to be specifically resisted and prayed against?
25. Is there anyone from outside the area we should consider bringing in to assist us with our strategy/planning/training/doing?
26. Should we be considering sending certain individuals on evangelism training (e.g. TIE Teams)?
27. Should we be restructuring our meetings or leadership to encourage evangelism?
28. *What does God have to say?*

Finally, let me stress a vital point on this five-part framework for developing a strategy for growth. Every aspect of the framework must be made to work at *each of the four levels of church life*. These four levels are necessary to healthy church growth, so your commitment/development/research/action/assessment must affect and be effective at the level of:

- single person—individual church member
- cell—the homegroup and the specialist Evangelism Teams, healthily 18–30 strong, with an optimum number for homegroups at twelve
- congregation—the incarnational means of culturally contextualising the gospel community into the world's community, healthily between 30 (for a new church plant) and 150 strong, with an optimum of 130, the exception being a

      reproducing mother church, whose membership
      needs to be around 200

- celebration—joining congregations of a sufficient size together to affect a whole city and to spread resources across congregations, initiating projects too big for any one congregation, but ensuring the links are through relationship and vision.

These then are the outlines of a framework arising from a basic theology of evangelism, with a few practical nuts and bolts thrown in to facilitate radical (or New Testament) whole-church evangelism. In closing it may be useful to summarise this *Perspective* of evangelism, taking us back to the roots of effective 'gospelling'.

CHAPTER 15

SUMMARY

1. God wants to communicate.
2. God communicates incarnationally.
3. God's incarnational communication is good news.
4. The mandate of proselytisation runs throughout Scripture—Old and New Testament.
5. New Testament evangelism is church-based, seeing the Great Commission as both fulfilled and enabled by disciples formed through church life.
6. New Testament evangelism plants churches, recognising the need for apostolic teams (including evangelists) as the best means of fulfilling the Great Commission.
7. New Testament evangelism involves the whole church in evangelism, whilst releasing the evangelist to do and to train.
8. Whole-church evangelism releases leadership bottle-neck and trains/develops new potential at a local church level.
9. Radical New Testament evangelism is Kingdom evangelism and therefore includes words, works and wonders.
10. It necessitates goals and strategies.
11. A church-based evangelism strategy demands a commitment from leadership and the whole church to communication of vision and to change.
12. It requires training and development at every level alongside research into target areas and people groups.

13. Action arising will affect the church's structures, finances, leadership team, meetings, homegroups and church calendar.
14. Action arising will also affect the community around that church through friendship and events evangelism, social action, profile and publicity, political action, targeting specific people groups, cold contacts, etc.
15. All of the above will be assessed regularly at each level (single, cell, congregation, celebration).

To close with the essential of the message, as Paul did when he concluded his letter to the church at Colossae in AD 62, radical evangelism could demand no better of us than to quote his words:

> Devote yourselves to prayer, being watchful and thankful. And pray for us, too, that God may open a door for our message, so that we may proclaim the mystery of Christ, for which I am in chains. Pray that I may proclaim it clearly, as I should. Be wise in the way you act towards outsiders; make the most of every opportunity. Let your conversation be always full of grace, seasoned with salt, so that you may know how to answer everyone.
>
> (Colossians 4:2–6)

RELATIONSHIPS— JESUS STYLE

Stuart Lindsell

For many of us, it is in the area of relationships that we feel the most insecure. Relating to God is not too bad, but relationships with people can be fraught with difficulties and misunderstanding.

This Pioneer *Perspective* is therefore focused on a word of instruction that Jesus spoke to His disciples about their relationships together. Jesus, by His words, His lifestyle of love, acceptance and forgiveness, His faith in His church and purity in His relationships, is our great example. Jesus also recognised His own need of others despite His unique relationship with the Father.

This useful book gives guidance to all of us in creating and maintaining relationships within the church. The biblical teaching is logical and here we have a powerful aid to uniting the church by building strong relationships based on love, acceptance, trust and respect.

Catalogue Number YB 9727   £3.99

PROPHECY IN THE CHURCH

Martin Scott

At key times prophecy can shape your life. It is a gift which can radically change the course of a person's life or even that of a nation. Helping, inspiring and blessing, the individual is touched by words from the very Father heart of God, spoken to you as an individual or to the church as the body of Christ.

This book in the Pioneer *Perspectives* series is primarily concerned with the gift of prophecy and also the role and ministry of the prophet, leading one to ask:

Does this affect me? Can the Holy Spirit really dwell within me? Should I be expectant and desire change and challenge?

Martin Scott clearly states the Holy Spirit does reside in the Christian and He can manifest Himself through you at the right time in a variety of situations. Prophecy happens because God is a person who speaks. It is simply one of the things that the Holy Spirit does when He is free to do as He wishes.

This book is a sound study aid as we learn to be aware of and expectant for the Holy Spirit. Prophecy is a gift which we should expect to be poured out liberally during the age of the Holy Spirit. So much so, that Paul expected us to 'eagerly desire spiritual gifts, especially the gift of prophecy' *(1 Cor. 14:1)*.

Catalogue Number YB 9726   £3.99

THE ROLE AND MINISTRY OF WOMEN

Martin Scott

This two-part study in the Pioneer *Perspectives* series is the result of faithful research into an emotive subject; the role of women in the church—specifically in relation to their ministry as leaders. In a topic of heated debate the author has related the role women should play in the light of the revelation of God found within His Word.

The author points out that the Gospel comes to liberate regardless of differing perspectives; it makes us into the men and women God wants us to be. In Christ there is full and equal redemption for all people regardless of race, gender or social background *(Gal. 3:28)*.

So, how can women best be freed to serve effectively as God wants? If there are questions which remain, let us deal with each other graciously, knowing that God is always willing to shed more light where we are seeking answers, which will help us continue to walk in integrity before Him.

Catalogue Number YB 9725   £3.99